Richard Murphy, an Æ Memorial Award winner, has spent the last two years in the West of Ireland, where he has restored the 'Ave Maria', the last Galway-built hooker, and sailed her off the Connemara coast. In this documentary poem he tells the history of his boat and presents a vivid record of a vanishing way of life.

5s.

RICHARD MURPHY: THE LAST GALWAY HOOKER

RICHARD MURPHY

THE LAST GALWAY HOOKER

THE DOLMEN PRESS

IN THE SUMMER OF 1952, I HAD A JOB guarding a salmon-river in the West of Ireland. If it rained heavily, the salmon were safe because the current would be too strong for the poachers' nets, and one could go away for a few days. My brother was on holiday in the district, and he had hired a sailing-boat of a local design known as a *pookhaun*. This *pookhaun* was a bad one. First, she had a bad reputation, because five men had been lost out of her in 1927 in what was called the Cleggan disaster. Second, because her bilges were sealed with cement, and her spars were on the point of breaking. However, we wanted a holi-day and we wanted to go to an island, in particular we wanted to go to Clare Island, a place full of legends. We

[5]

never got there. Contrary winds brought us to Inishbofin instead.

Many years after that holiday, which I described in a
poem called "Sailing to an Island", I returned to Inishbofin for a much longer visit, two years ago, and since
then the island has become my home. Admirers of
D. H. Lawrence's short story, "The Man who Loved
Islands", may smile at the awful hazards: first, investing
in island property: last, moving out of the main island
onto a smaller one where the only inhabitant is oneself.
I fell victim to both lures: firstly, by buying a boat,
which was as much as I could afford; and lastly, by
living on it. The boat I bought was larger than a
pookhaun. She was old, solid, cow-like from some
angles, but strangely beautiful. An outmoded trawler or
drifter whose engine had failed, she came into the
harbour at Inishbofin on her brown sails and I had to
make a deal.

She was called the *Ave Maria*, and curiously enough,
the superstition which used to bar women from having
anything to do with boats was flouted in her building.
A woman had planked her. This glorious exception, the
Ave Maria, was a hooker, that is, a strong, safe, fishing
and cargo boat designed before the age of engines to
sail the dangerous sounds between mainland and islands
off the Galway coast. She had been launched on the
Claddagh, the old fishing village at the gates of Galway
City, in 1922, the year of the Civil War in Ireland, and
she was the last hooker to be built there. She is one
of a very few that are still in commission. In its heyday

a hundred and fifty years ago the Claddagh fleet numbered about five hundred hookers, disciplined under its own mayor. Fire used to be carried in these boats, not only for cooking: if any poachers, meaning boats from elsewhere, were found in Galway Bay on the fishing-grounds, their gear was thrown overboard and the craft burnt. Last summer, there was only one hooker at the Claddagh docks which was still fishing under sail with hand-lines and no engine. The inshore fishing has been wiped out by powerful modern trawlers.

The boatwright who built the *Ave Maria* is described as "tasty" in the Galway sense of a craftsman who does both skilled and polished work. The trade name "Ailsa Craig" belongs to a popular make of diesel engine. "Spillets" (also called "spillers") are long fishing-lines with a hundred or more hooks, and "trammels" are nets used locally for catching baits for the spillets and the lobster pots.

INISHBOFIN CO. GALWAY 1960   R.M.

Where the Corrib river chops through the Claddagh
To sink in the tide-race its rattling chain
The boatwright's hammer chipped across the water

Ribbing this hooker, while a reckless gun
Shook the limestone quay-wall, after the Treaty
Had brought civil war to this fisherman's town.

That "tasty" carpenter from Connemara, Cloherty,
Helped by his daughter, had half-planked the hull
In his eightieth year, when at work he died,

And she did the fastening, and caulked her well,
The last boat completed with old Galway lines.
Several seasons at the drift-nets she paid

In those boom-years, working by night in channels
With trammel and spillet and an island crew,
Tea-stew on turf in the pipe-black forecastle,

Songs of disasters wailed on the quay
When the tilt of the water heaves the whole shore.
"She was lucky always the *Ave Maria*",

With her brown barked sails, and her hull black tar,
Her forest of oak ribs and the larchwood planks,
The cavern-smelling hold bulked with costly gear,

Fastest in the race to the gull-marked banks,
What harbour she hived in, there she was queen
And her crew could afford to stand strangers drinks,

Till the buyers failed in nineteen twenty-nine,
When the cheapest of fish could find no market,
Were dumped overboard, the price down to nothing,

Until to her leisure a fisher priest walked
By the hungry dockside, full of her name,
Who made a cash offer, and the owners took it.

Then like a girl given money and a home
With no work but pleasure for her man to perform
She changed into white sails, her hold made room

For hammocks and kettles, the touch and perfume
Of priestly hands. So now she's a yacht
With pitch-pine spars and Italian hemp ropes,

Smooth-running ash-blocks expensively bought
From chandlers in Dublin, two men get jobs
Copper-painting her keel and linseeding her throat,

While at weekends, nephews and nieces in mobs
Go sailing on picnics to the hermit islands,
Come home flushed with health having hooked a fewdabs.

Munich, submarines, and the war's demands
Of workers to feed invaded that party
Like fumes of the diesel the dope of her sails,

When the Canon went east into limed sheep-lands
From the stone and reed patches of lobstermen
Having sold her to one on Cleggan Quay,

Who was best of the boatsmen from Inishbofin,
She his best buy. He shortened the mast, installed
A new "Ailsa Craig", made a hold of her cabin,

Poured over the deck thick tar slightly boiled;
Every fortnight he drained the sump in the bilge
"To preserve the timbers". All she could do, fulfilled.

The sea, good to gamblers, let him indulge
His fear when she rose winding her green shawl
And his pride when she lay calm under his pillage:

And he never married, was this hooker's lover,
Always ill-at-ease in houses or on hills,
Waiting for weather, or mending broken trawls:

Bothered by women no more than by the moon,
Not concerned with money beyond the bare need,
In this boat's bows he sheathed his life's harpoon.

A neap-tide of work, then a spring of liquor
Were the tides that alternately pulled his soul,
Now on a pitching deck with nets to hand-haul,

Then passing Sunday propped against a barrel
Winding among words like a sly helmsman
Till stories gather around him in a shoal.

She was Latin blessed, holy water shaken
From a small whiskey bottle by a surpliced priest,
Madonnas wafered on every bulkhead,

Oil-grimed by the diesel, and her luck lasted
Those twenty-one years of skill buoyed by prayers,
Strength forged by dread from his drowned ancestors.

She made him money, and again he lost it
In the fisherman's fiction of turning farmer:
The cost of timber and engine spares increased,

Till a phantom hurt him, ribs on a shore,
A hull each tide rattles that will never fish,
Sunk back in the sand, a story finished.

We met here last summer, nineteen fifty-nine,
Far from the missiles, the moon-shots, the money,
And we drank looking out on the island quay,

When his crew were in London drilling a motorway.
Old age had smoothed his barnacled will
And with wild songs he sold me the *Ave Maria*.

Then he was alone, stunned like a widower—
Relics and rowlocks pronging from the wall,
A pot of boiling garments, winter everywhere,

Especially in his bones, watching things fall,
Hooks of three-mile spillets, trammels at the foot
Of the unused double-bed—his mind threaded with all

The marline of his days twined within that boat,
His muscles' own shackles then staying the storm
Which now snap to bits like frayed thread.

So I chose to renew her, to rebuild, to prolong
For a while the spliced yards of yesterday.
Carpenters were enrolled, the ballast and the dung

Of cattle he'd carried lifted from the hold,
The engine removed, and the stale bilge scoured.
De Valera's daughter hoisted the Irish flag

At her freshly adzed mast this Shrove Tuesday,
Stepped while afloat between the tackle of the *Topaz*
And the *St. John*, by Bofin's best boatsmen,

All old as himself. Her skilful sail-maker,
Her inherited boatwright, her dream-tacking steersman
Picked up the tools of their interrupted work,

And in memory's hands this hooker was restored.
Old men my instructors, and with all new gear
May I handle her well down tomorrow's sea-road.

INISHBOFIN, CO. GALWAY
1960

Set in Perpetua type and printed in the Republic of
Ireland at the Dolmen Press, 23 Upper Mount Street
Dublin. *The Last Galway Hooker* is included in Richard
Murphy's volume of poems *Sailing to an Island* published
by Faber & Faber.

First printed May 1961
Second edition May 1962

THE LAST GALWAY HOOKER

is included in Richard Murphy's

volume of Poems

SAILING TO AN ISLAND

 er & Faber

12*s*. 6*d*.

CPSIA information can be obtained
at www.ICGtesting.com
Printed in the USA
BVHW050806140223
658473BV00005B/166